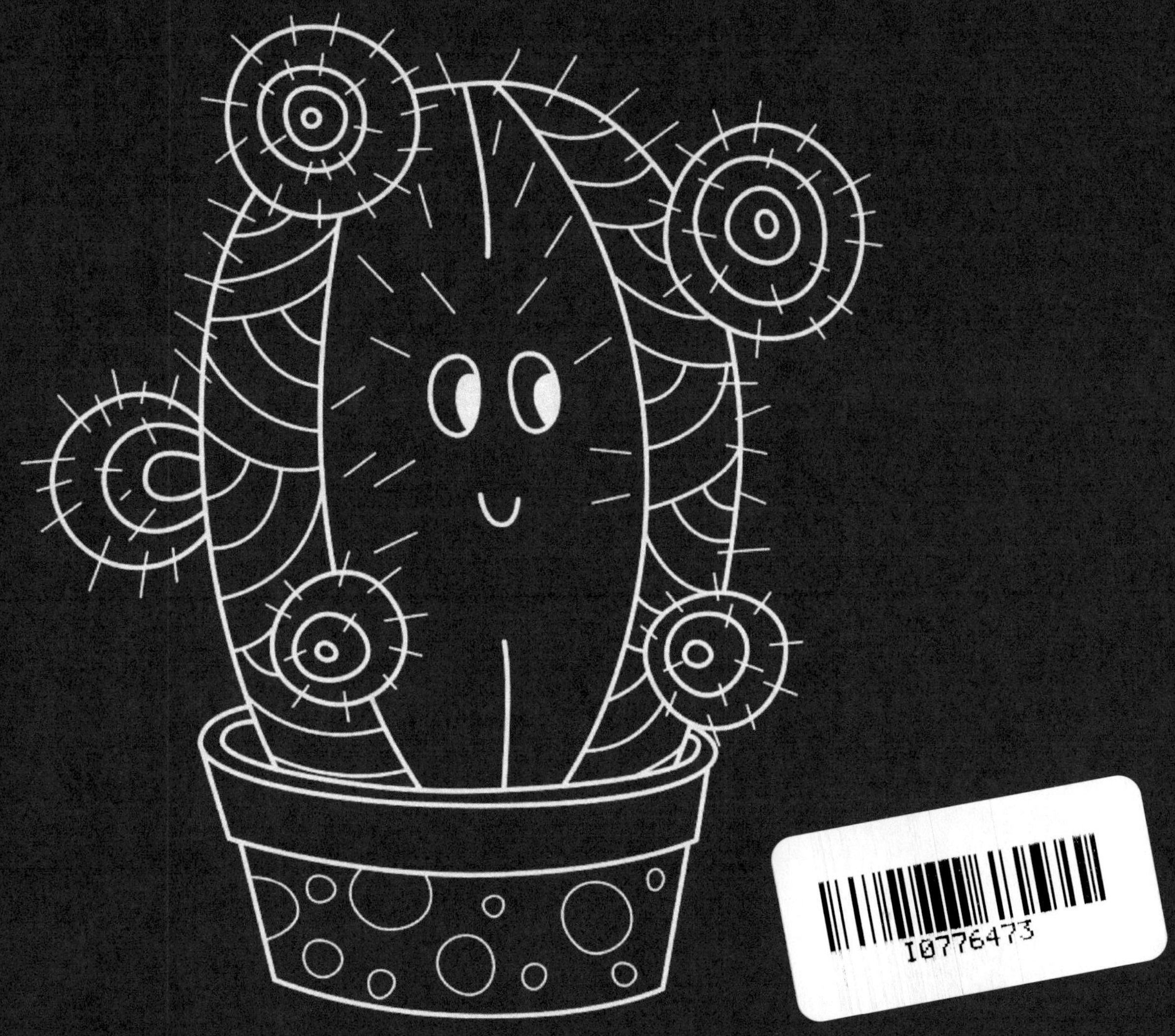

TINY CACTUS PUBLISHING

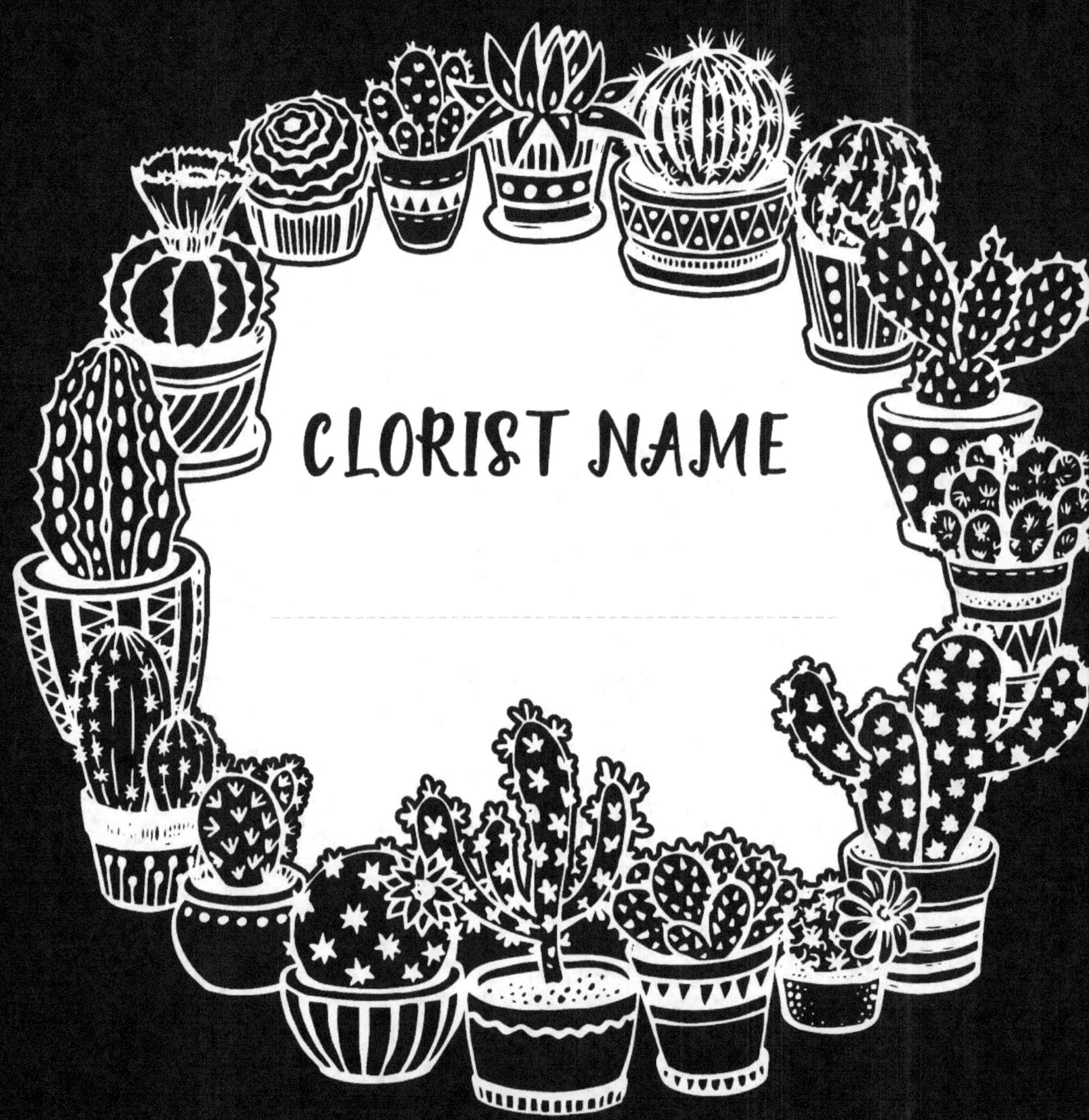
CLORIST NAME

TEST PAGE
PREPARE YOUR COLOR

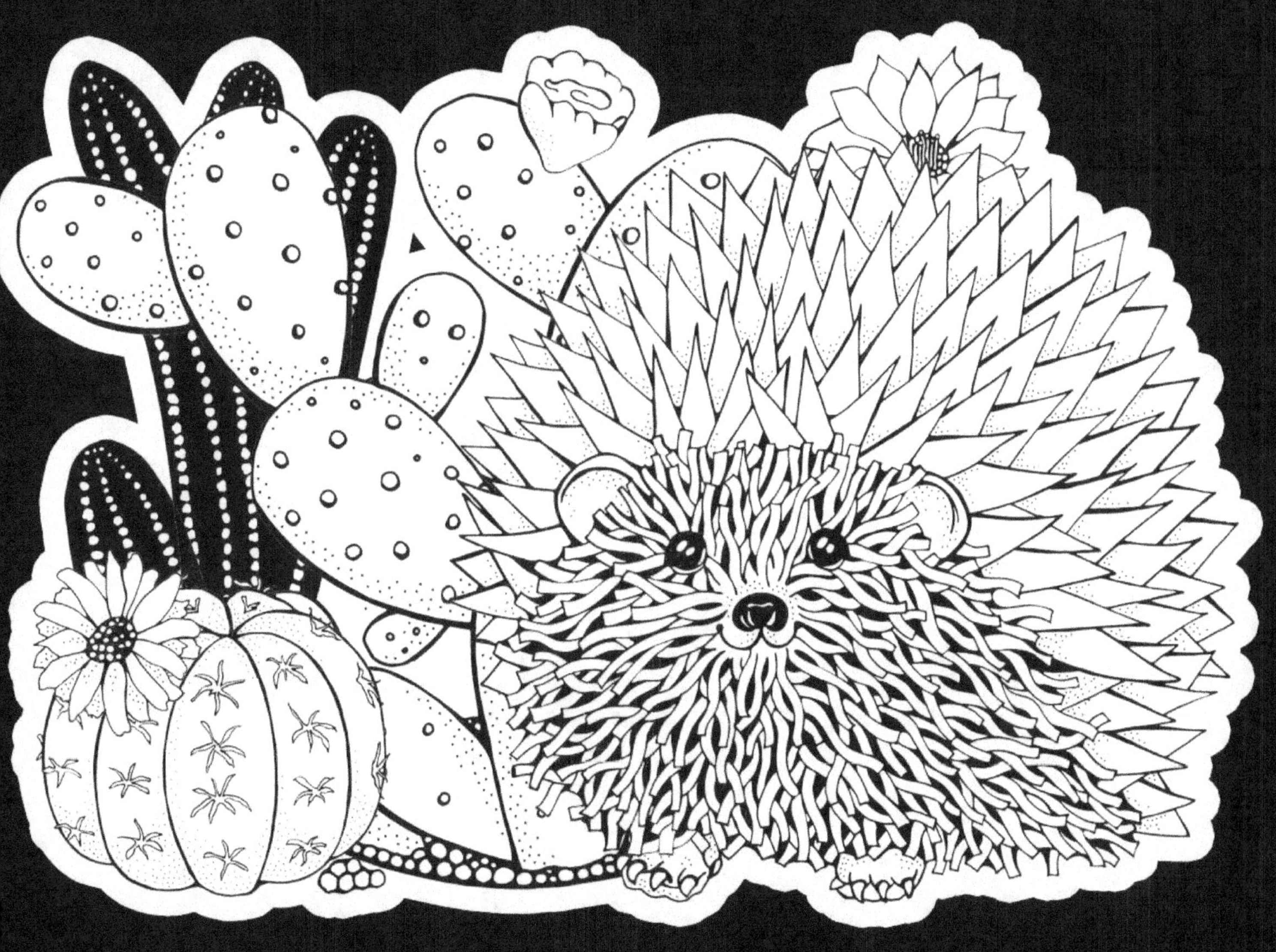

WARM UP !!

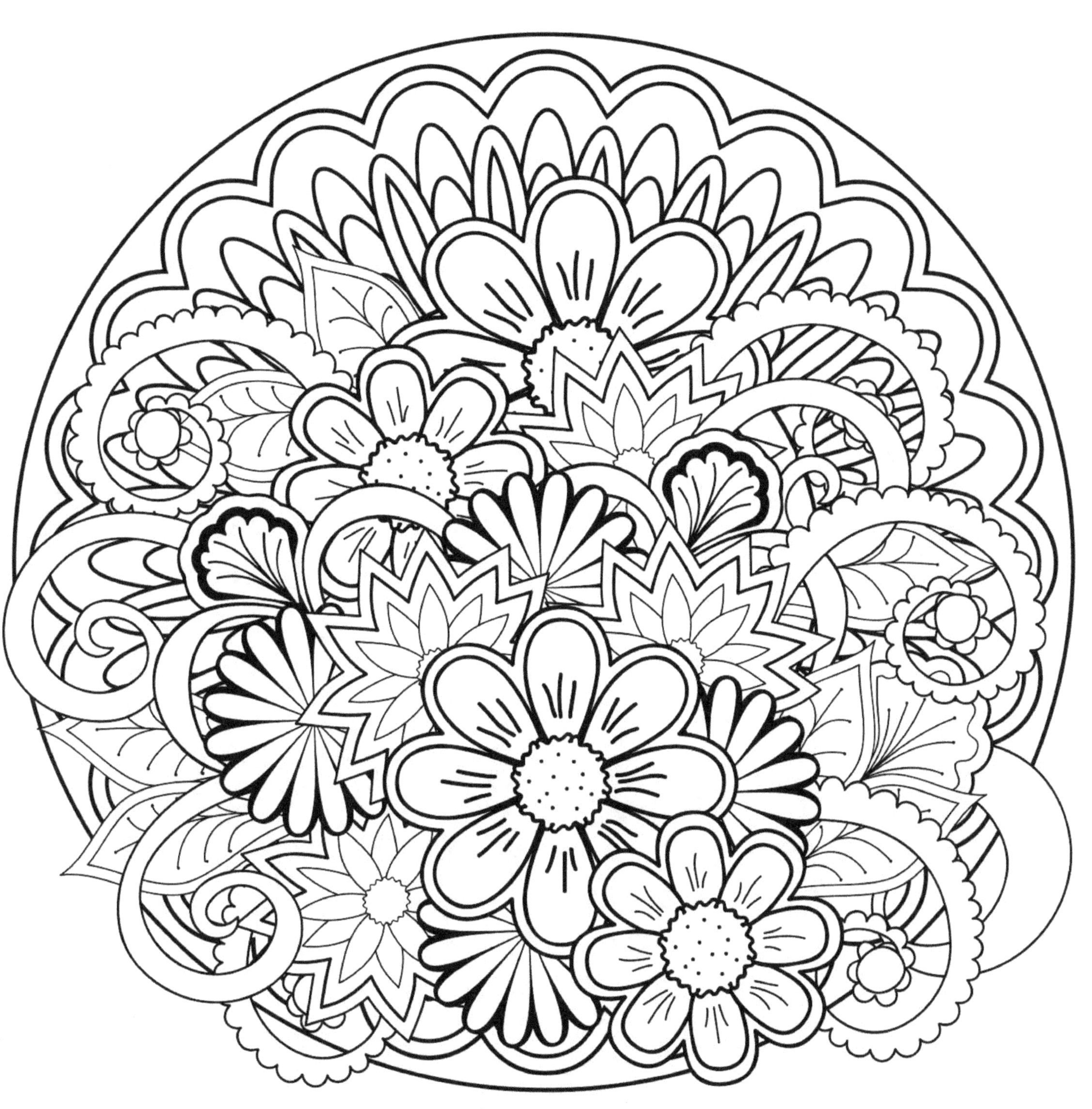

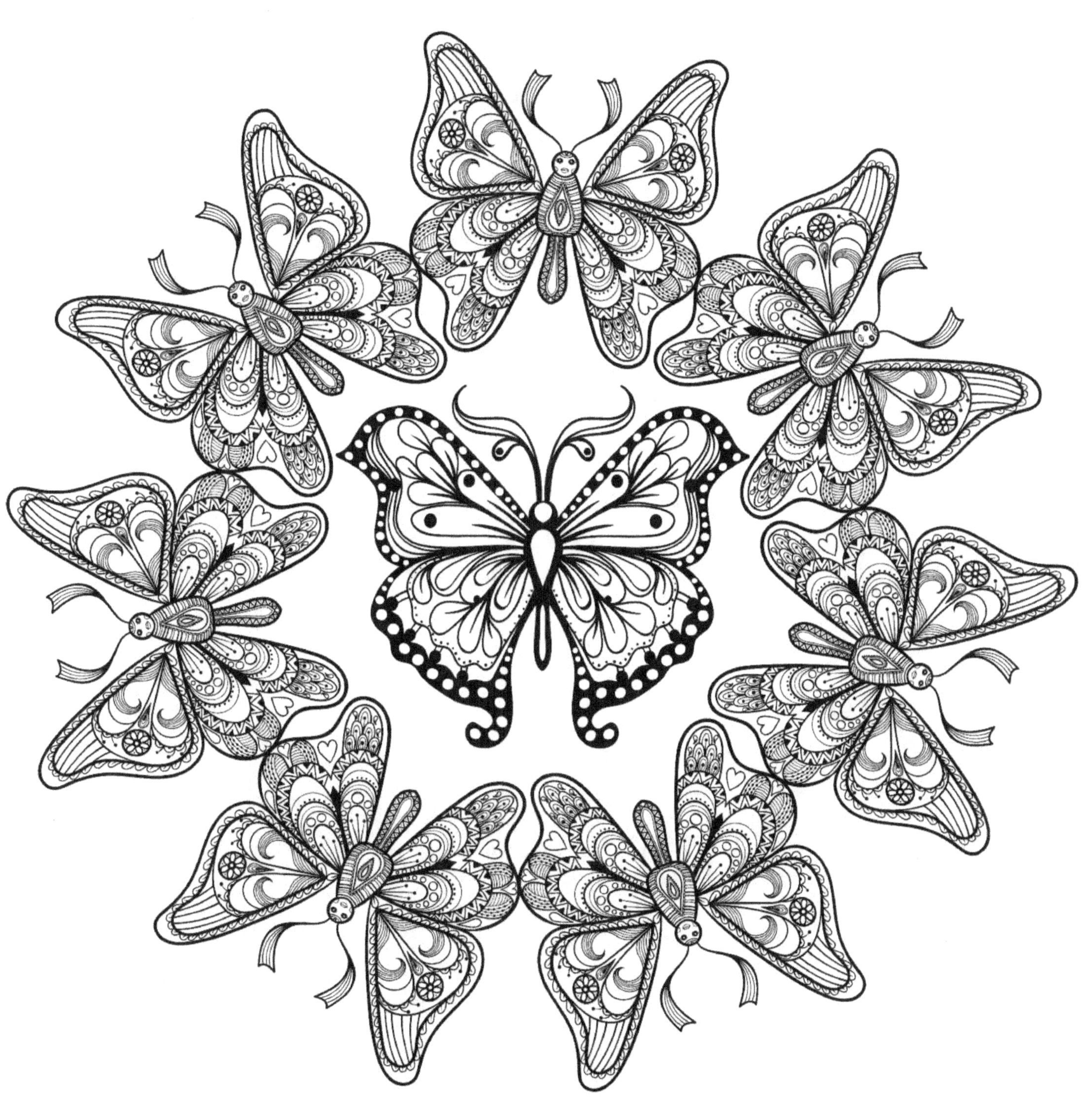

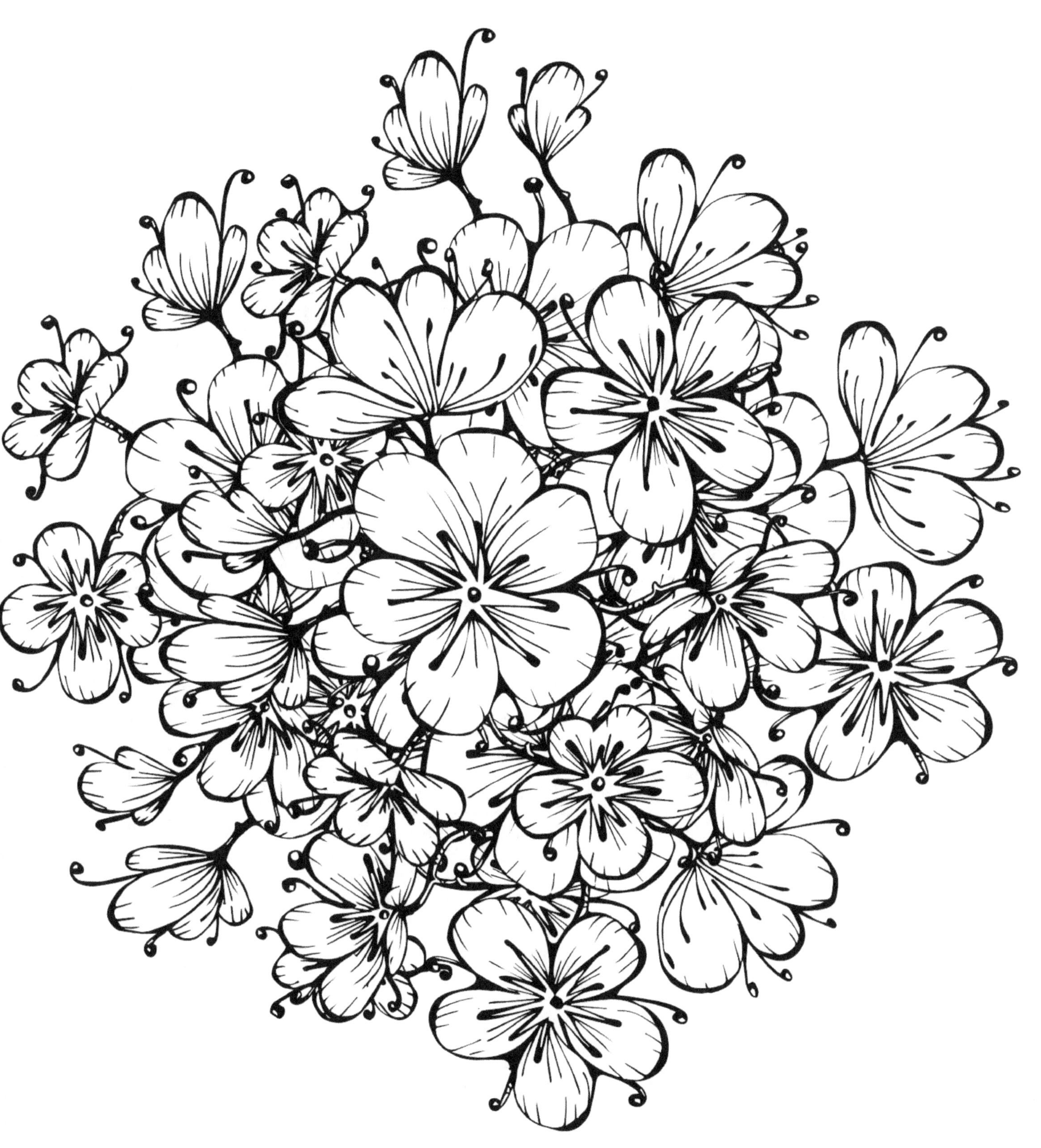

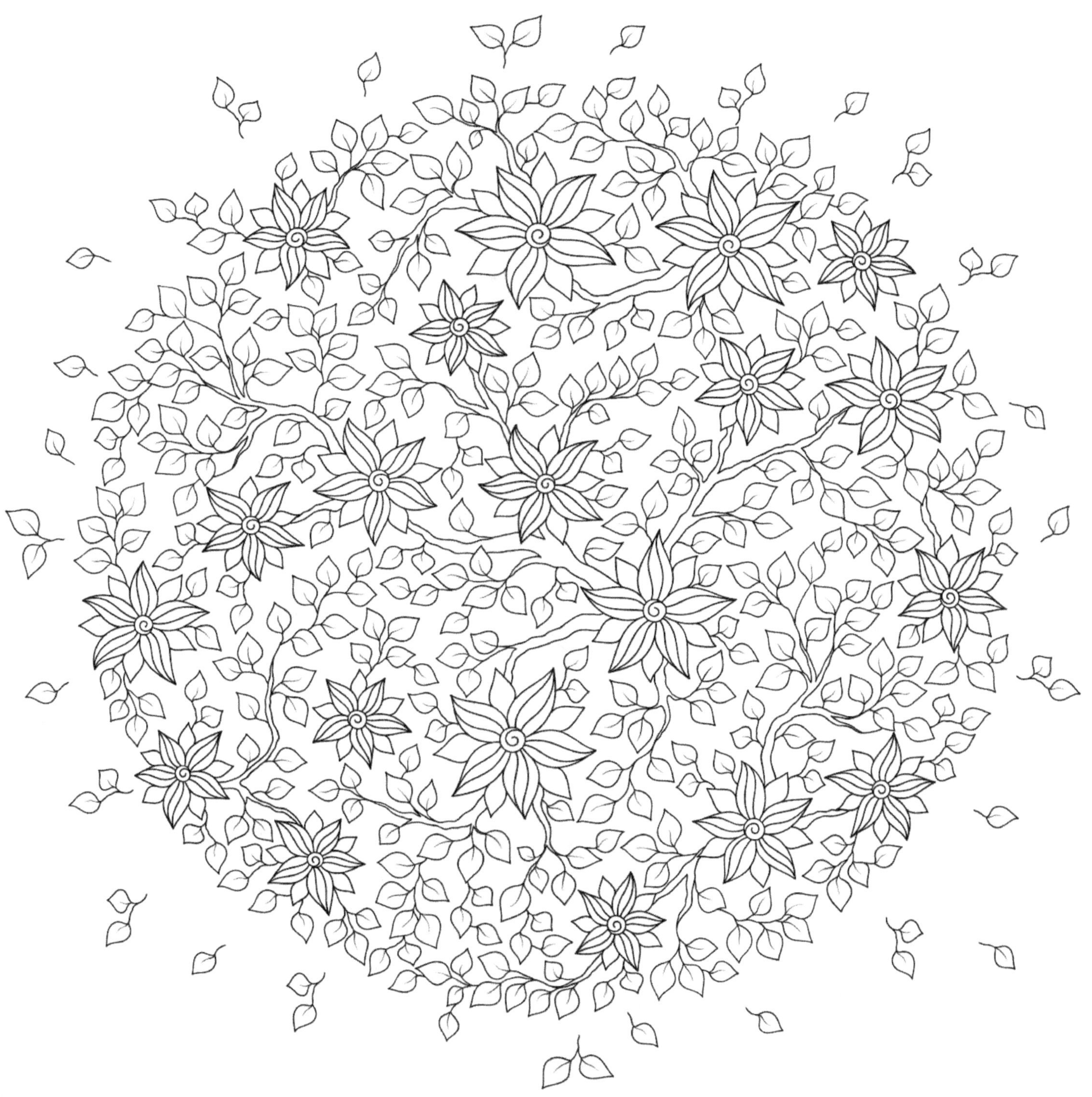

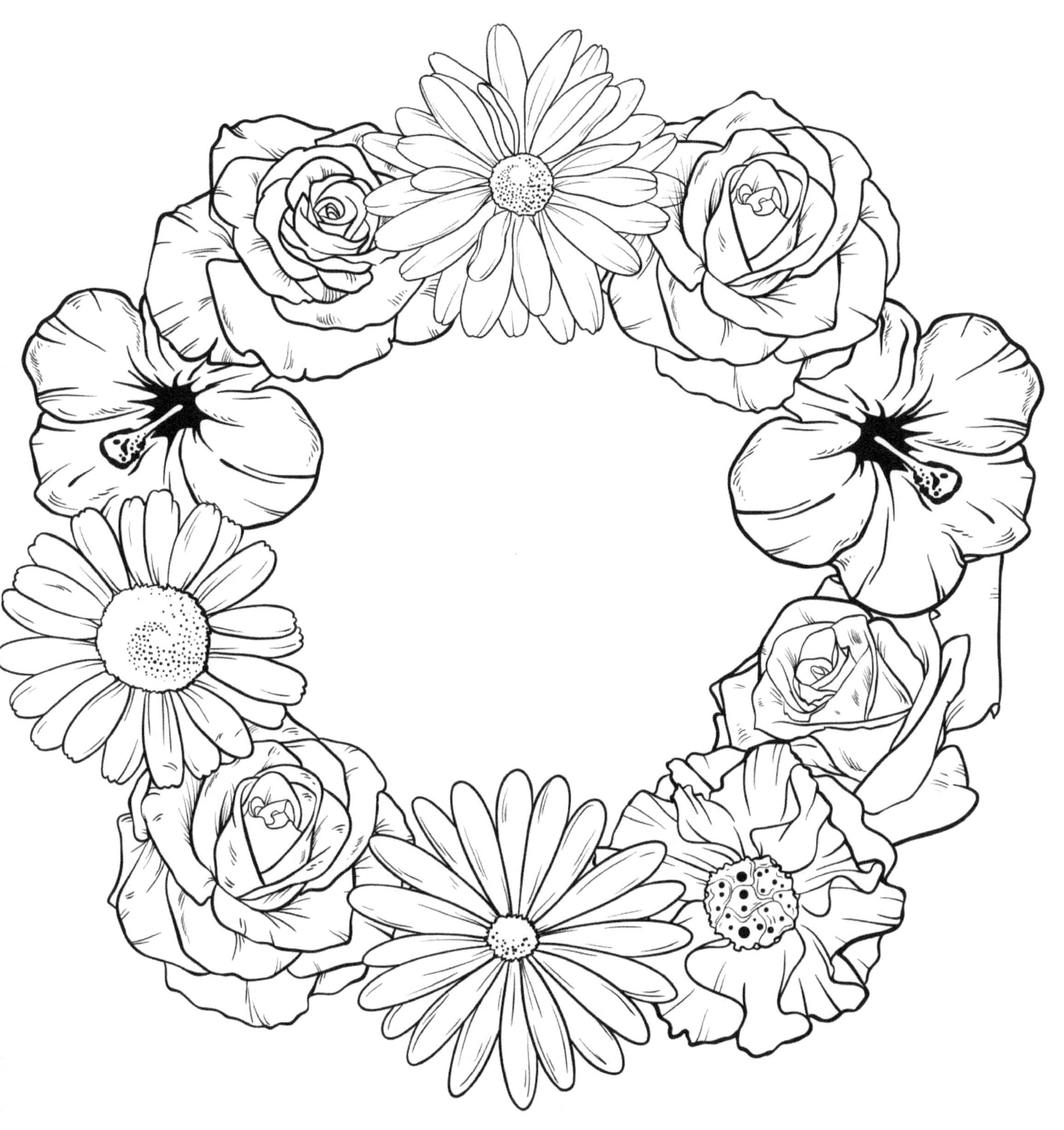

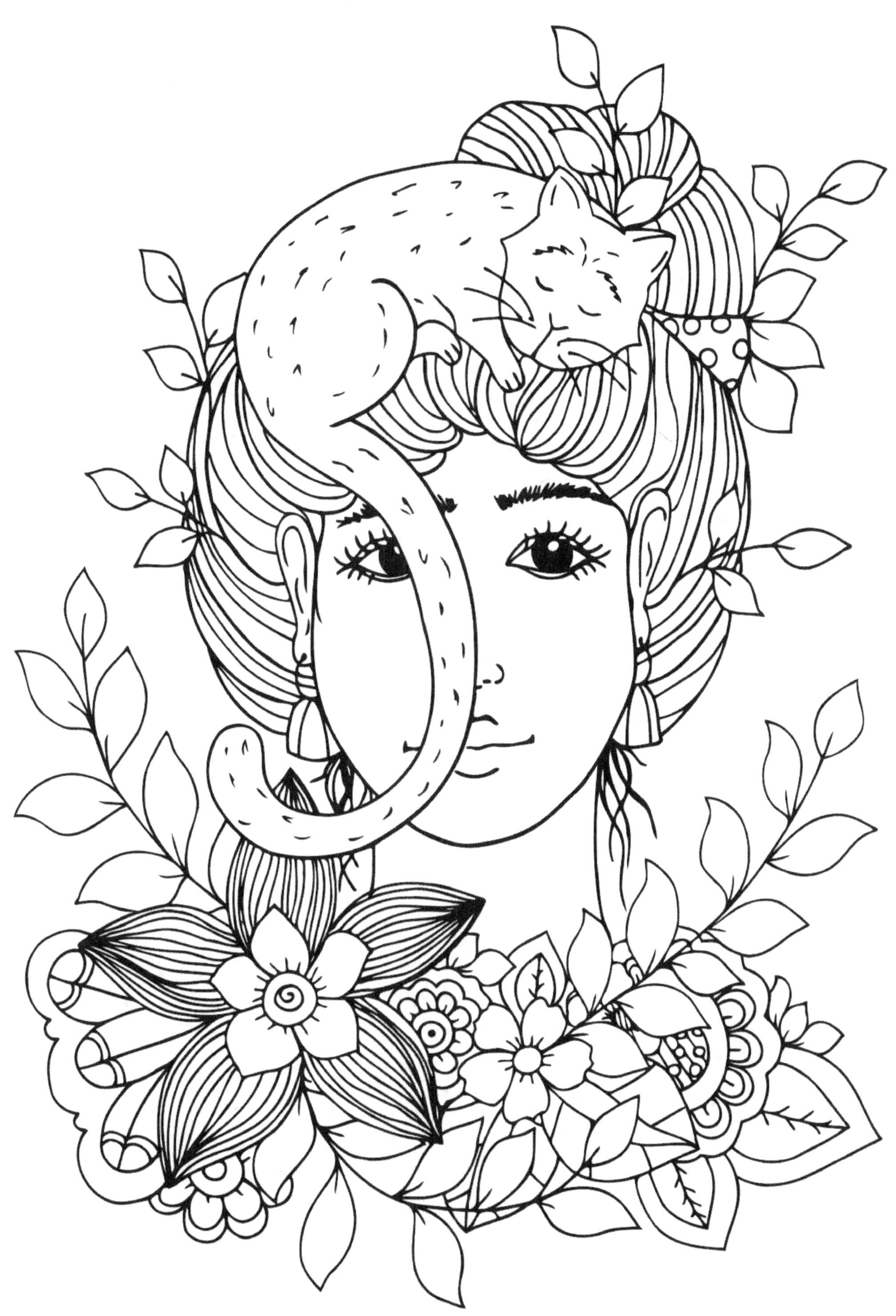

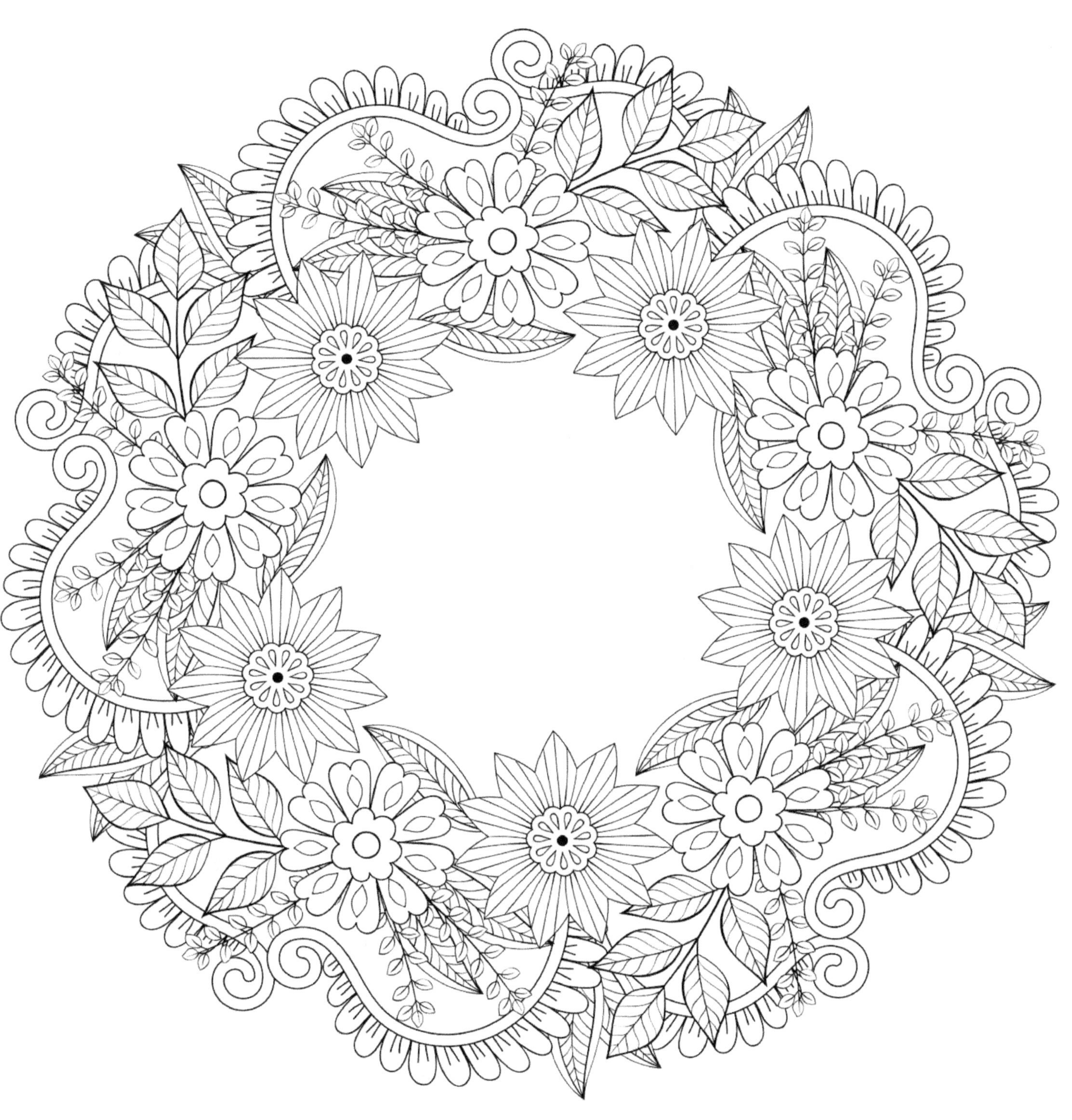

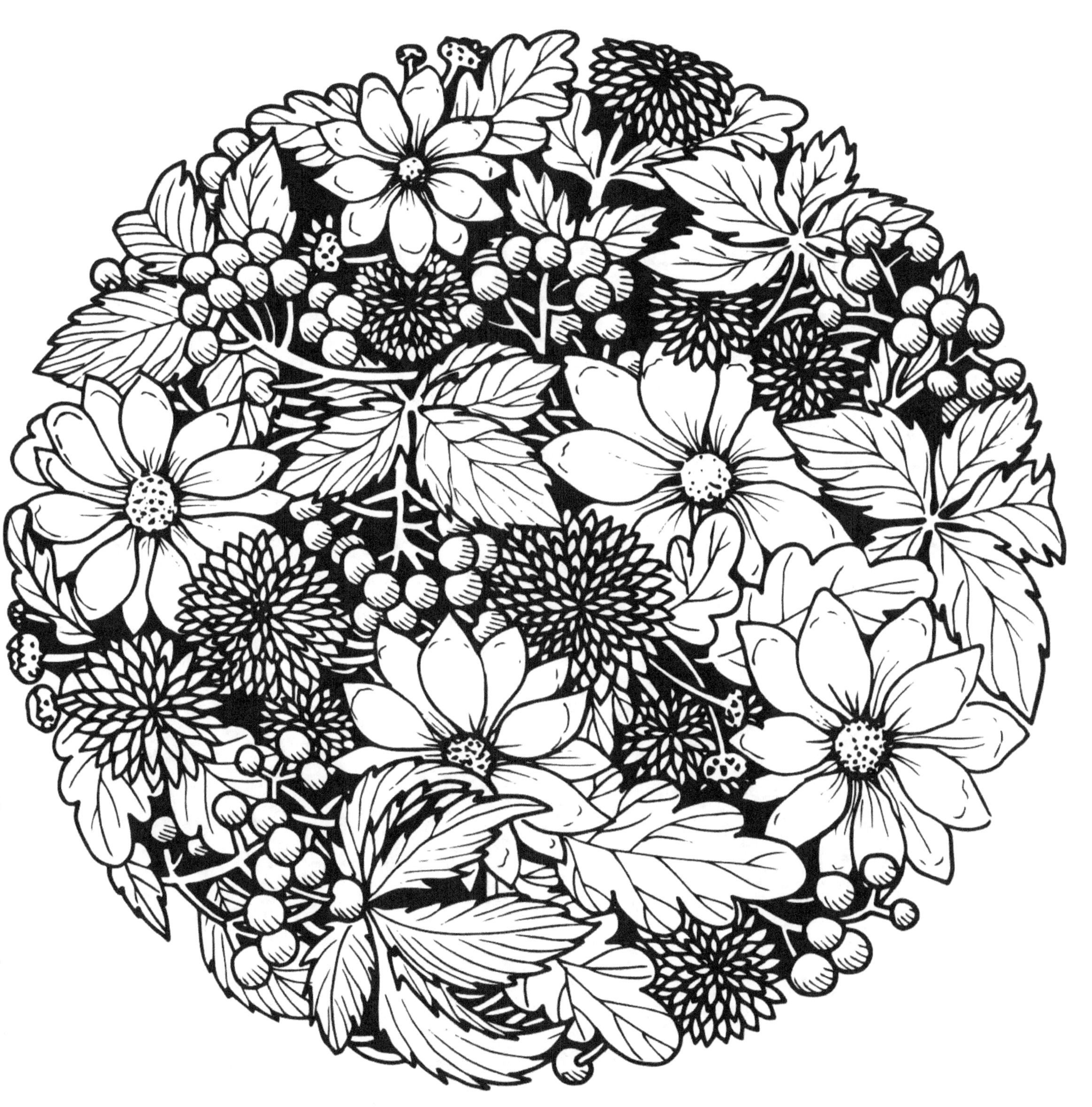

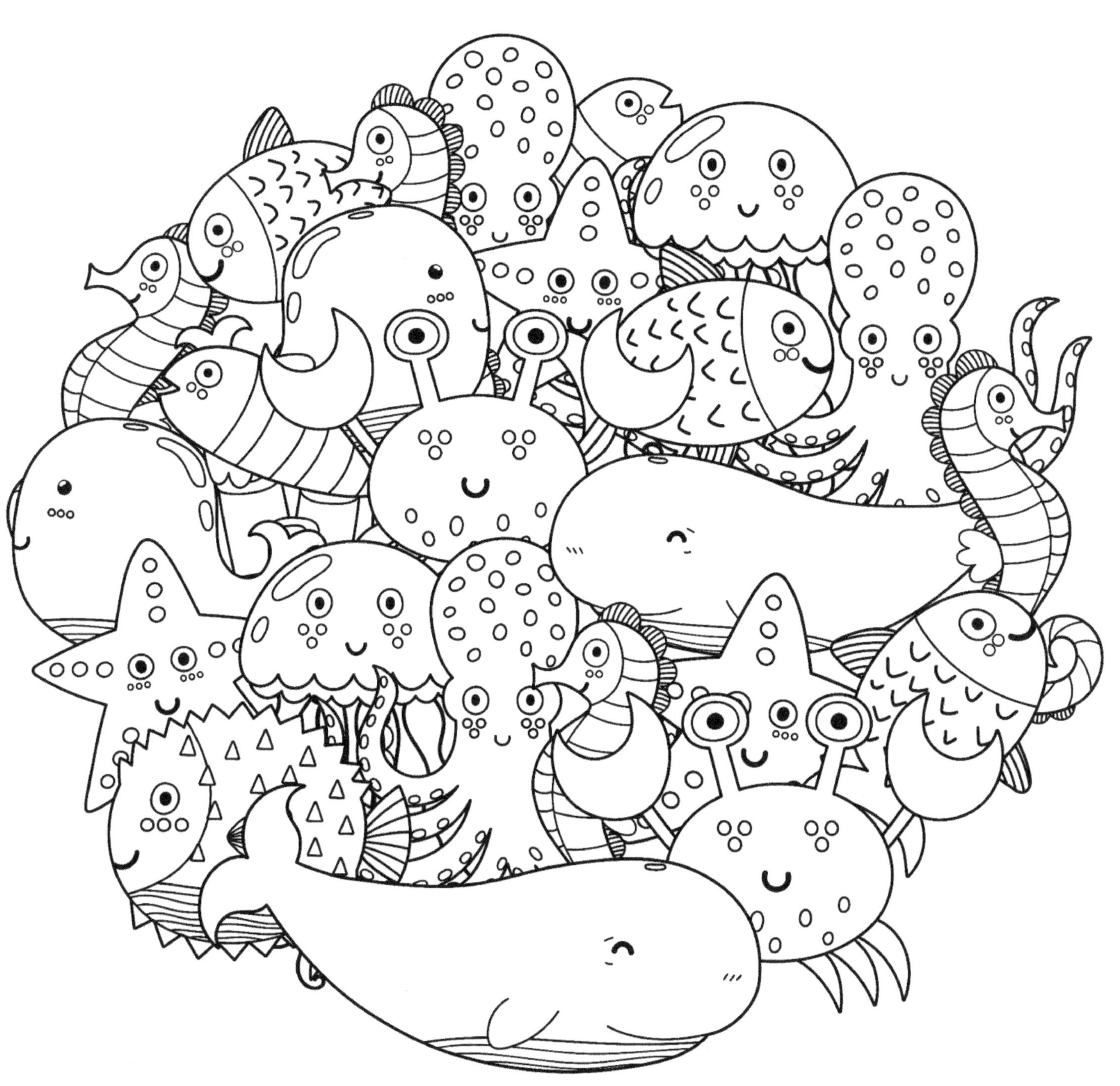

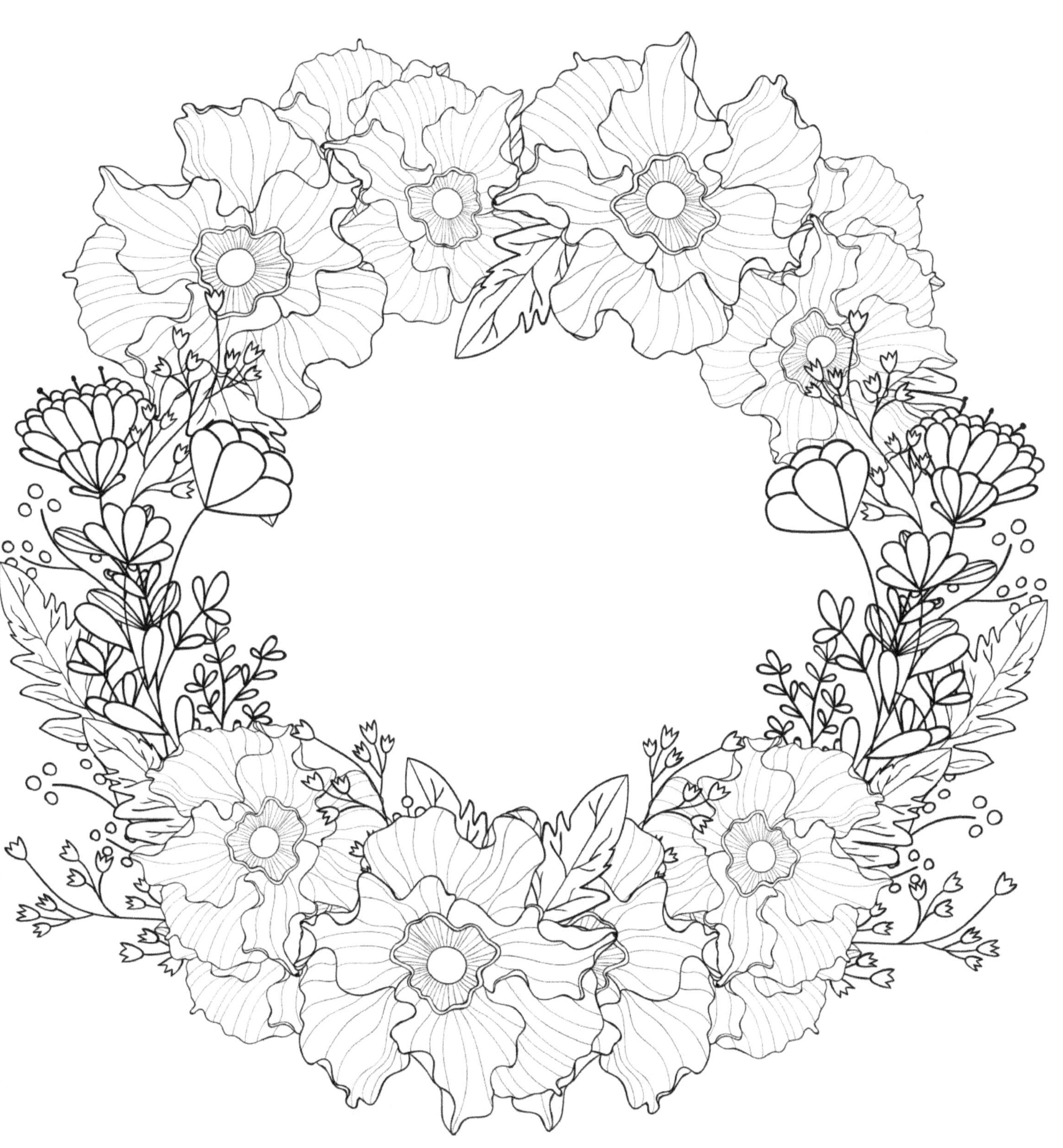

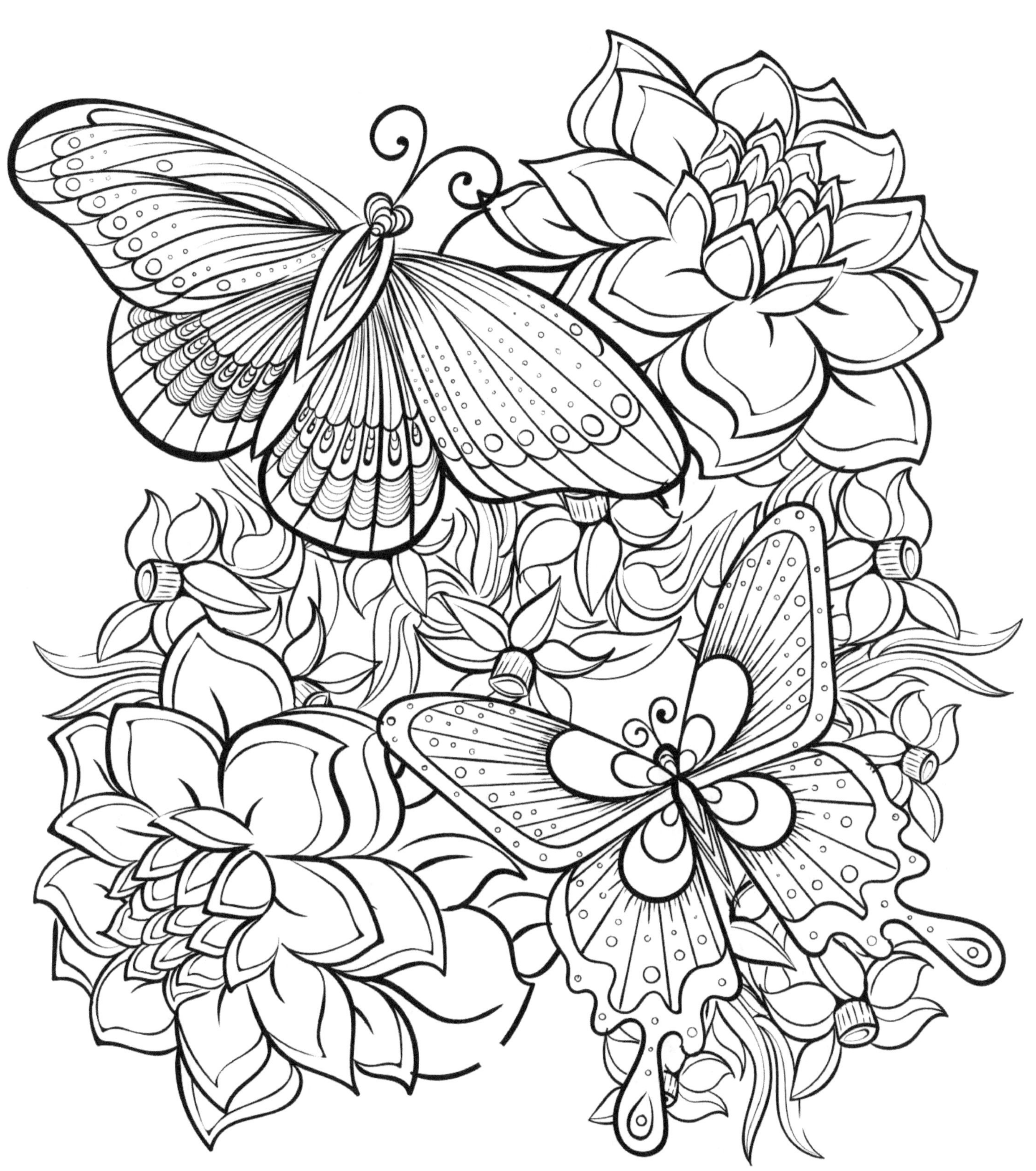

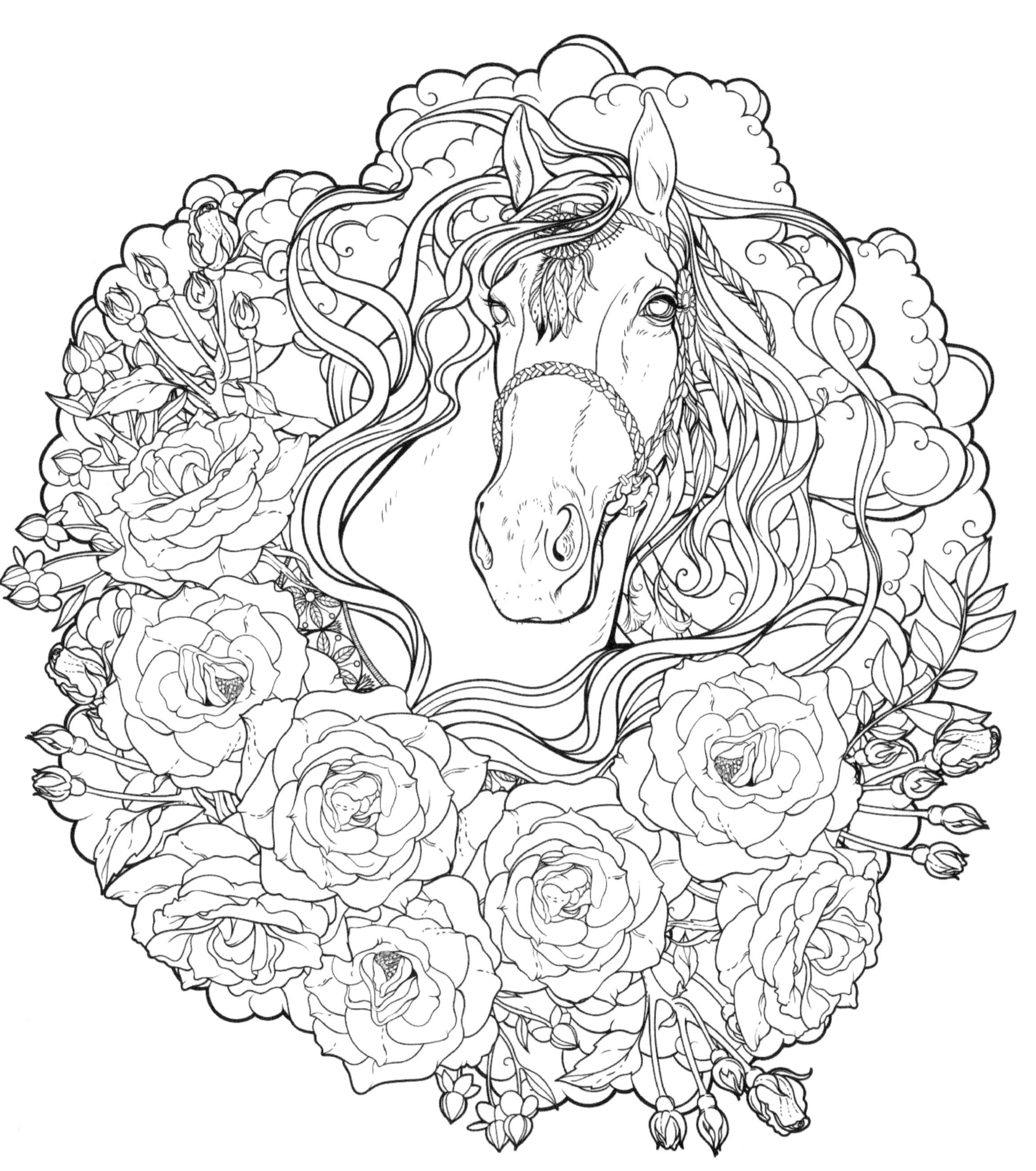

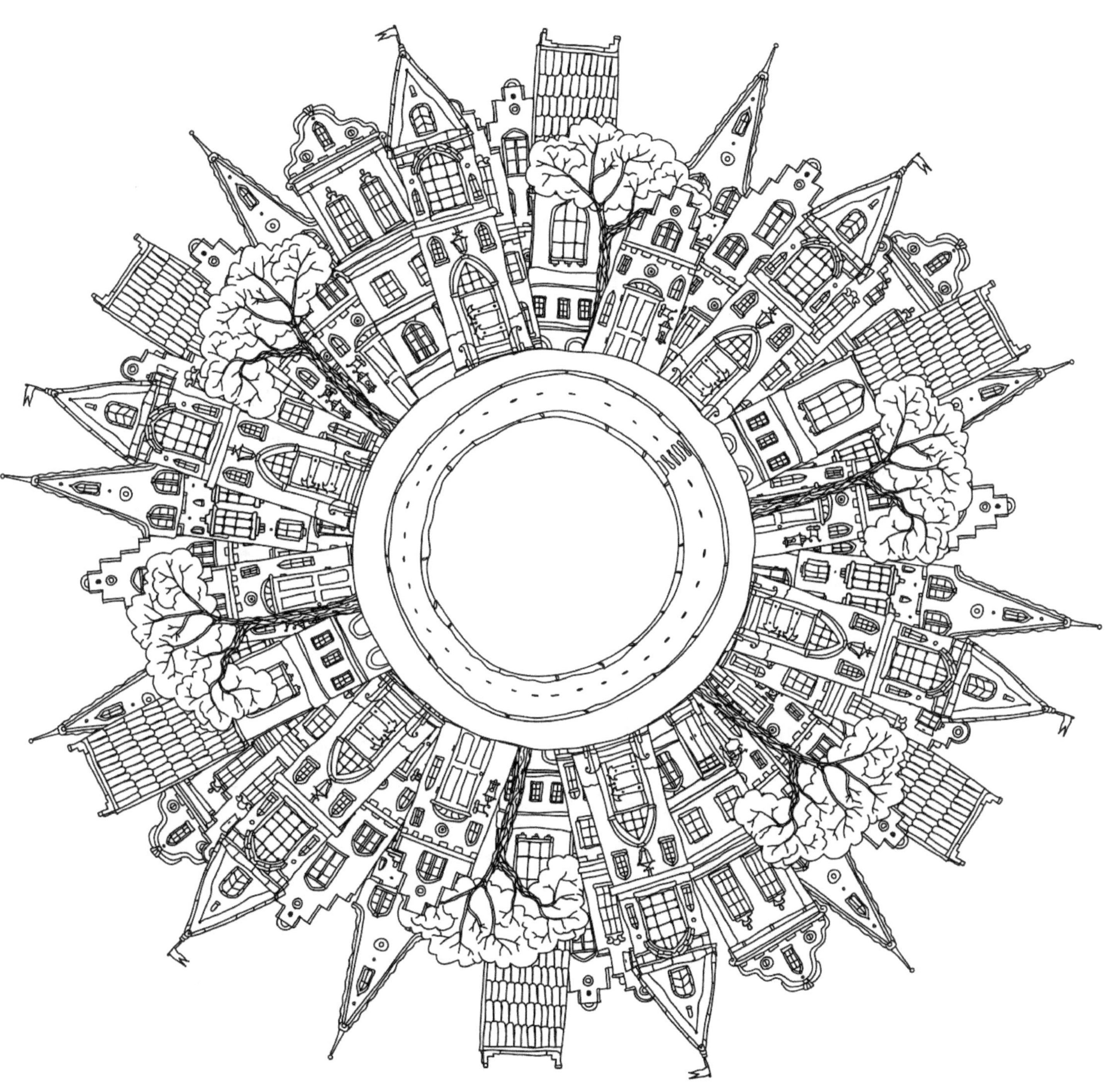

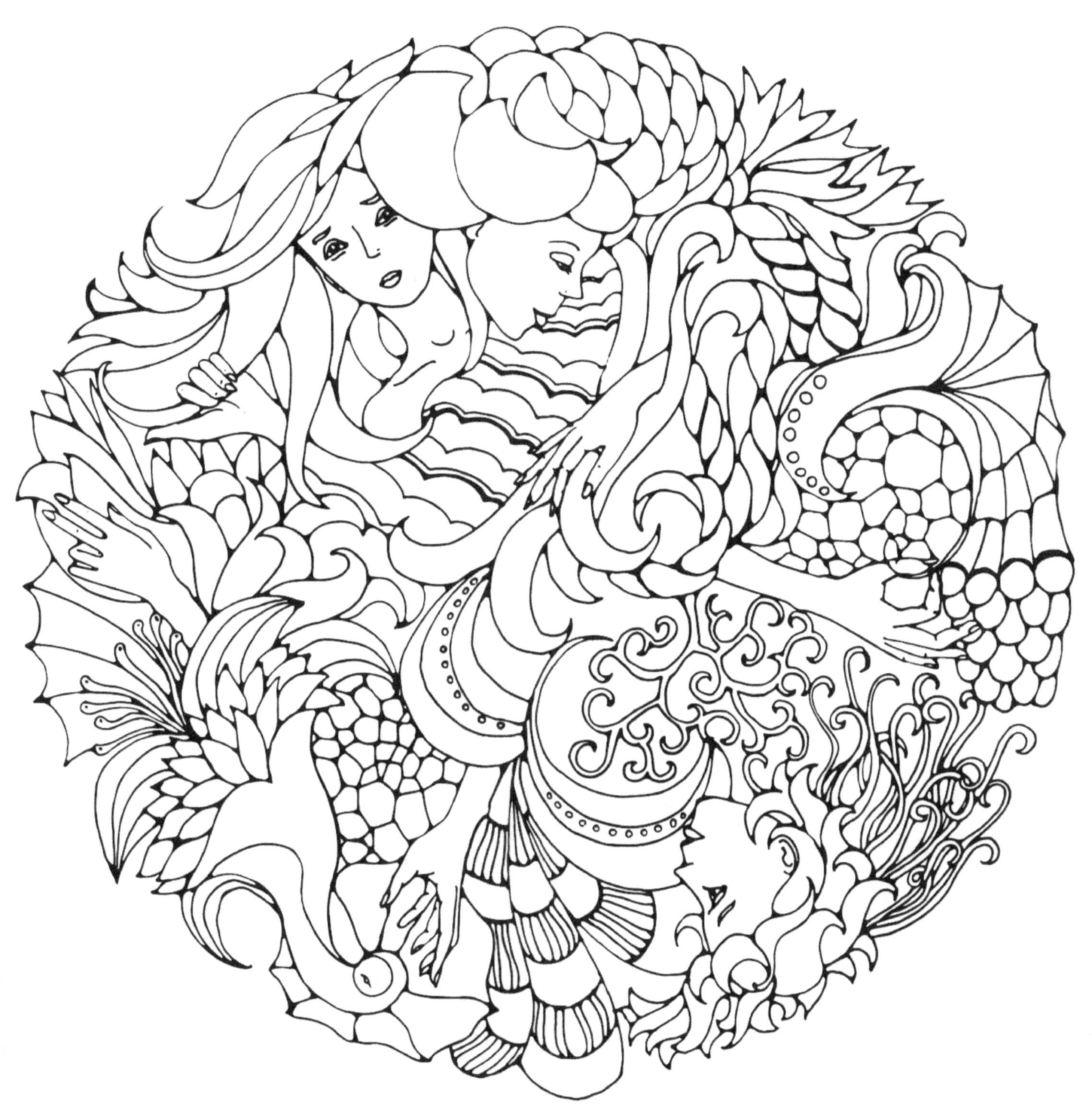

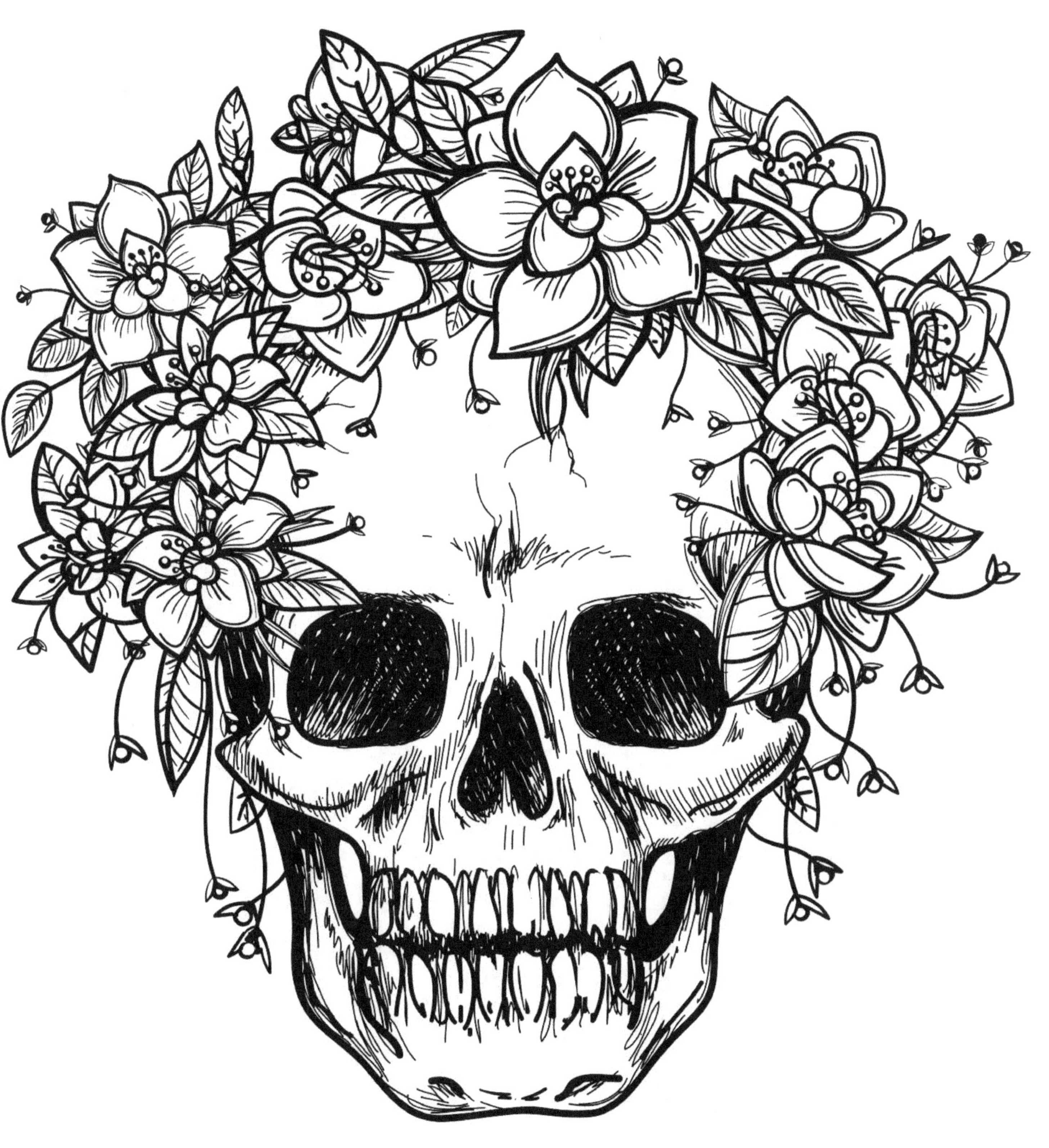

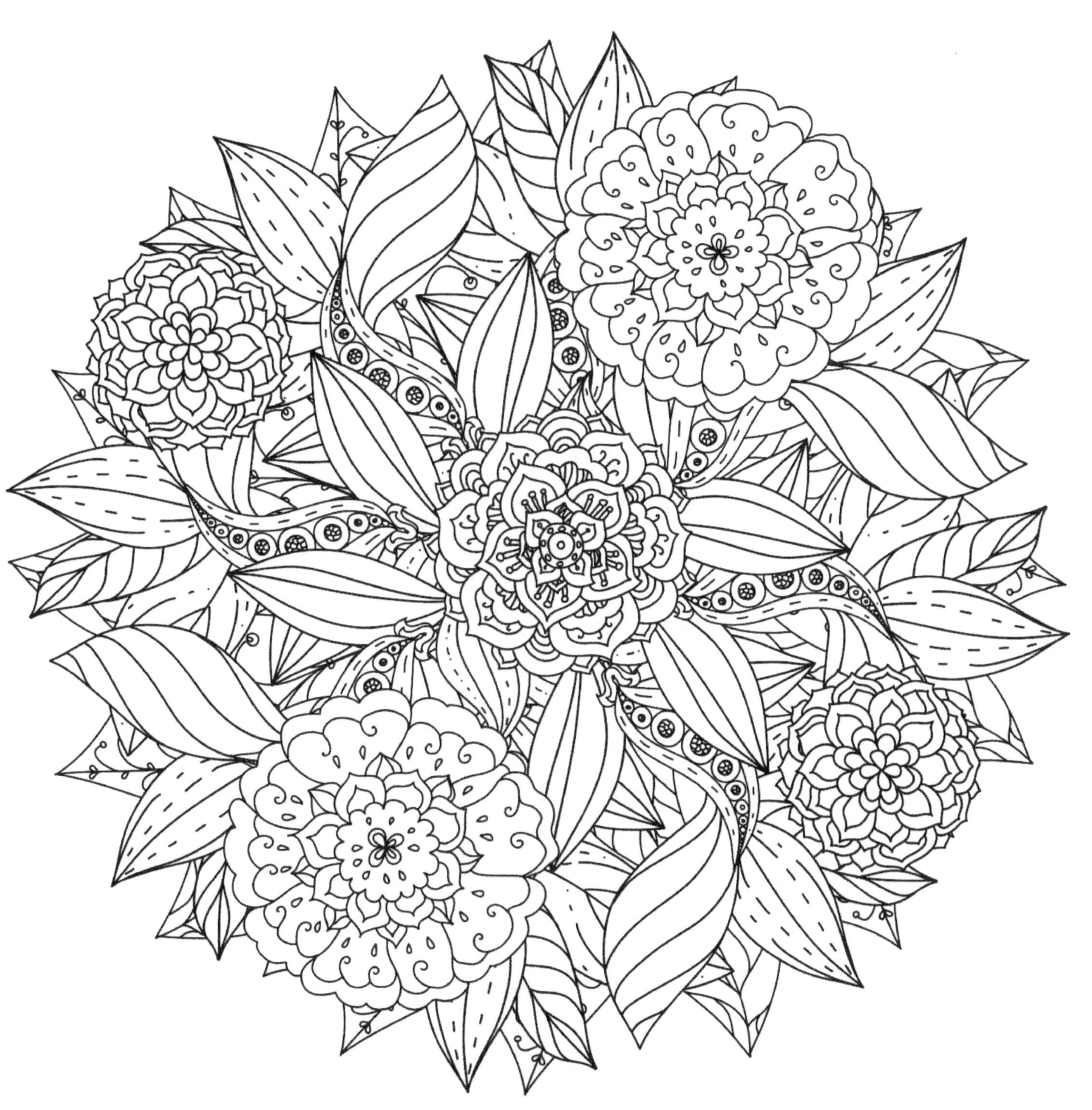

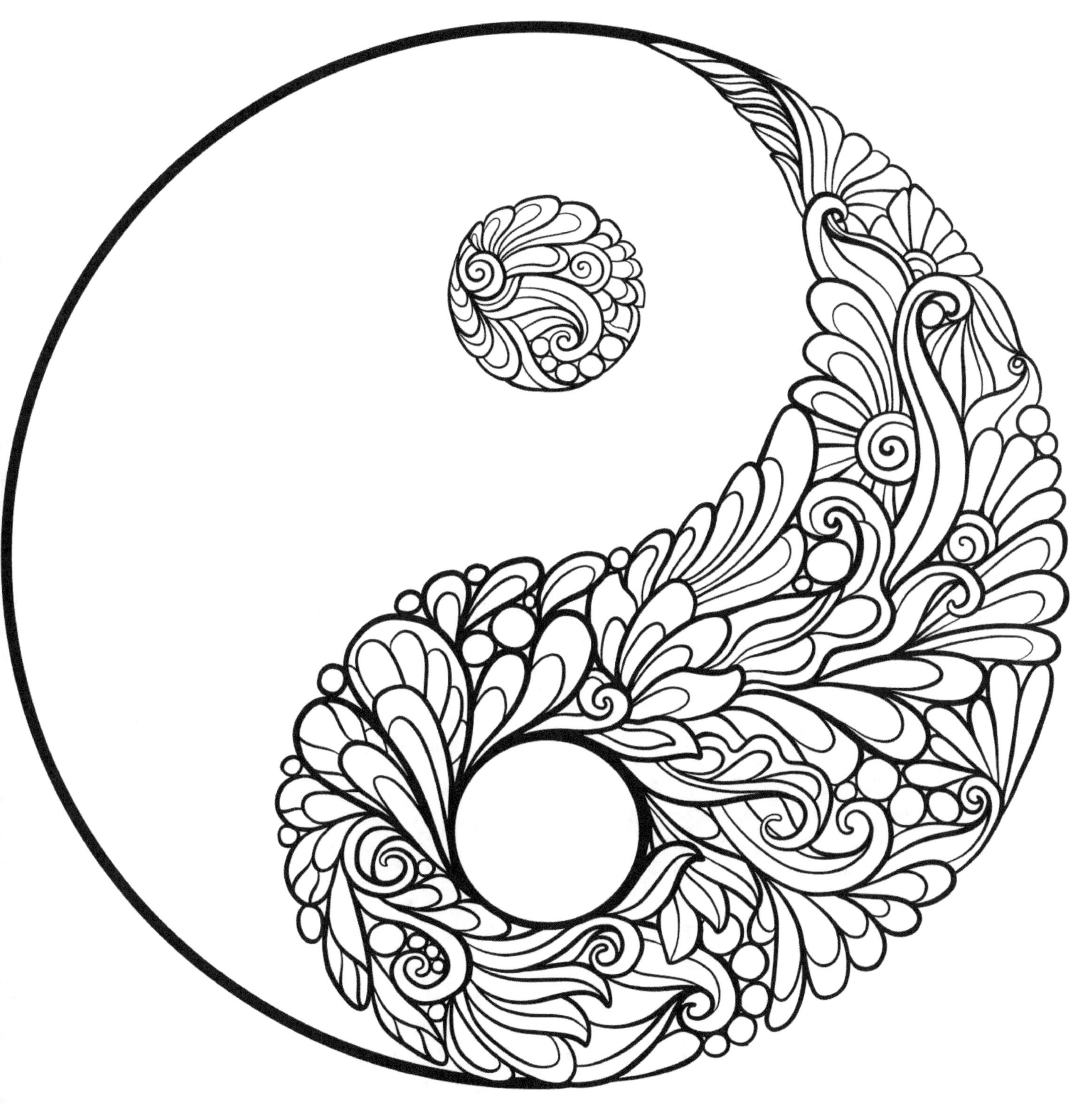

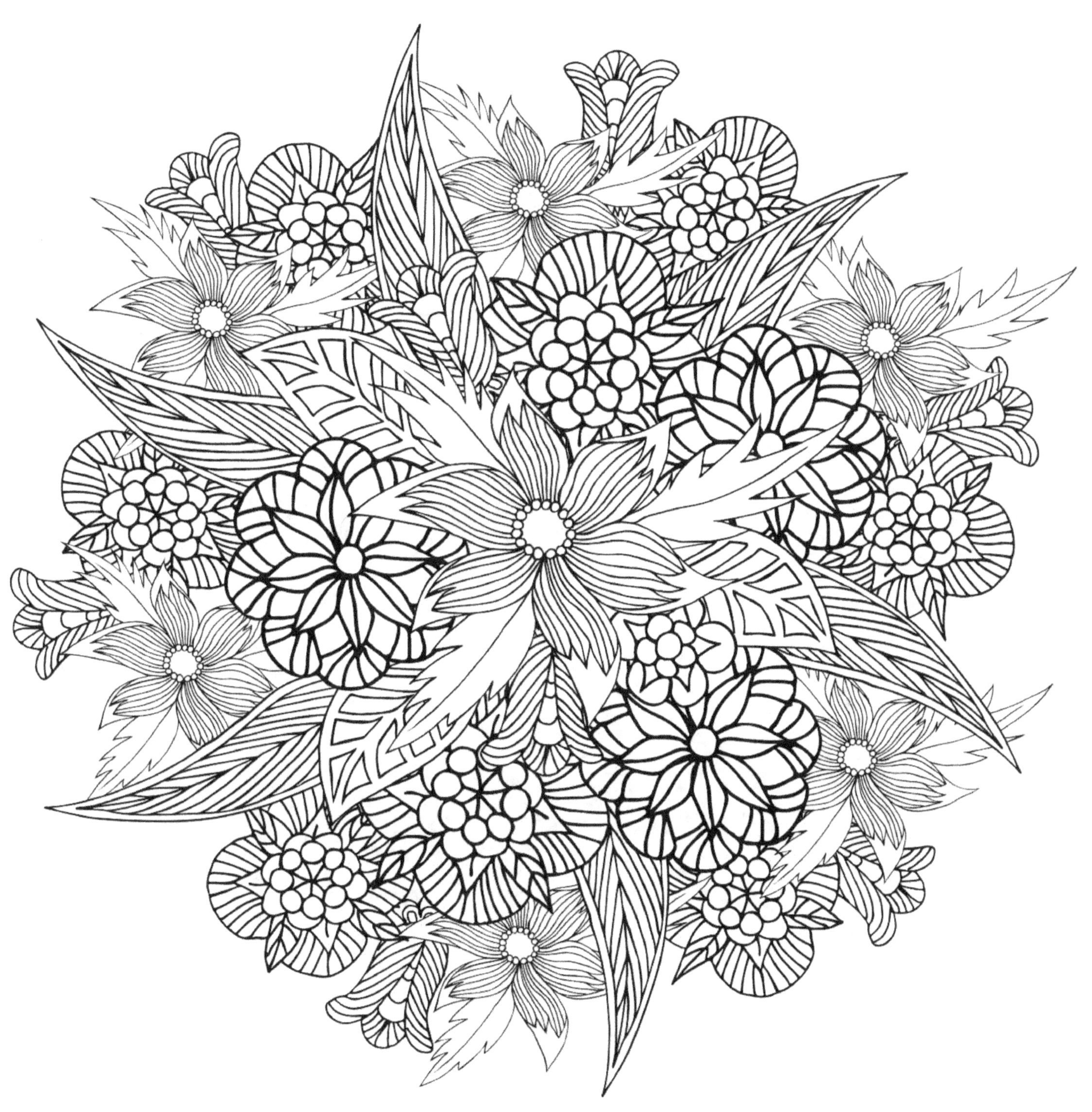

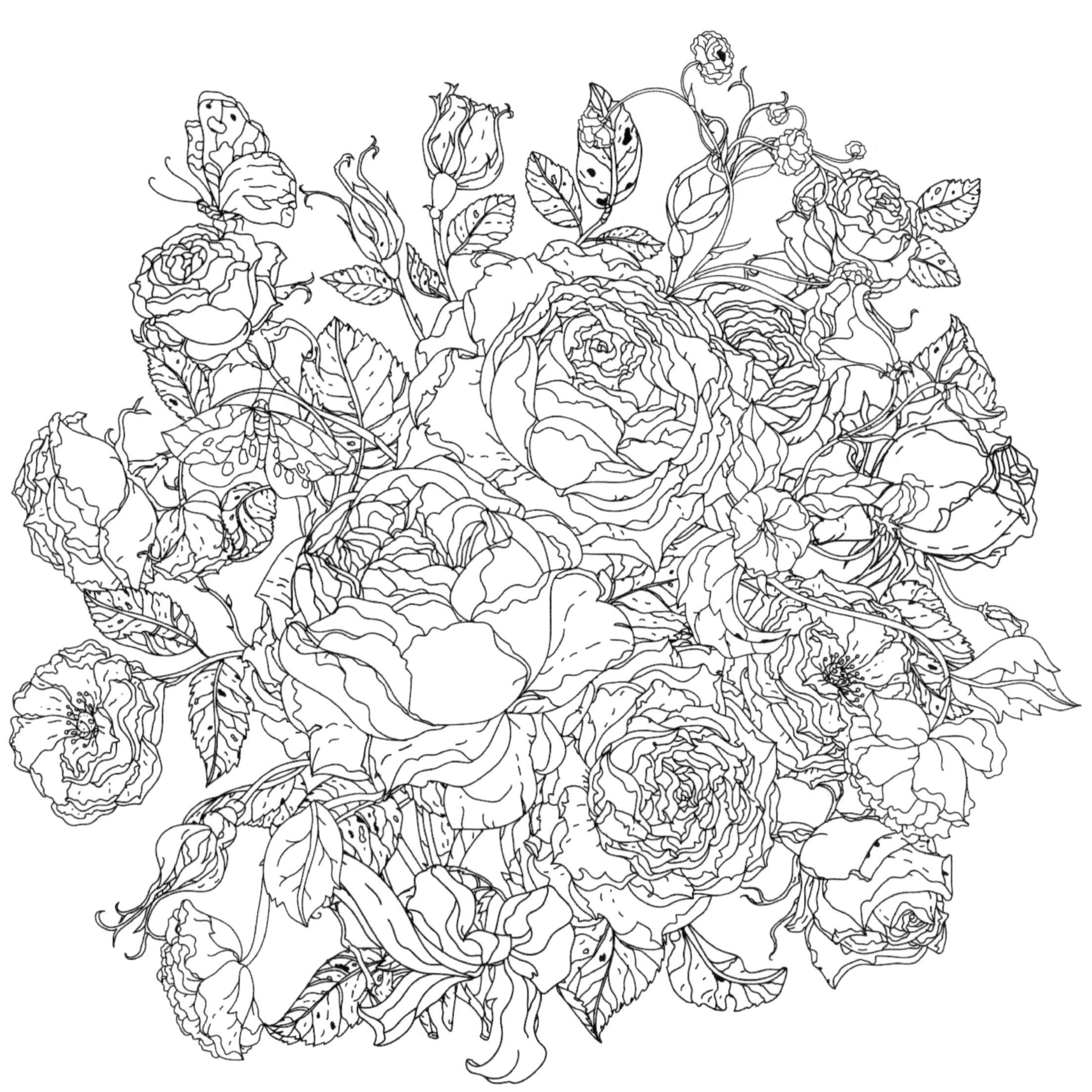

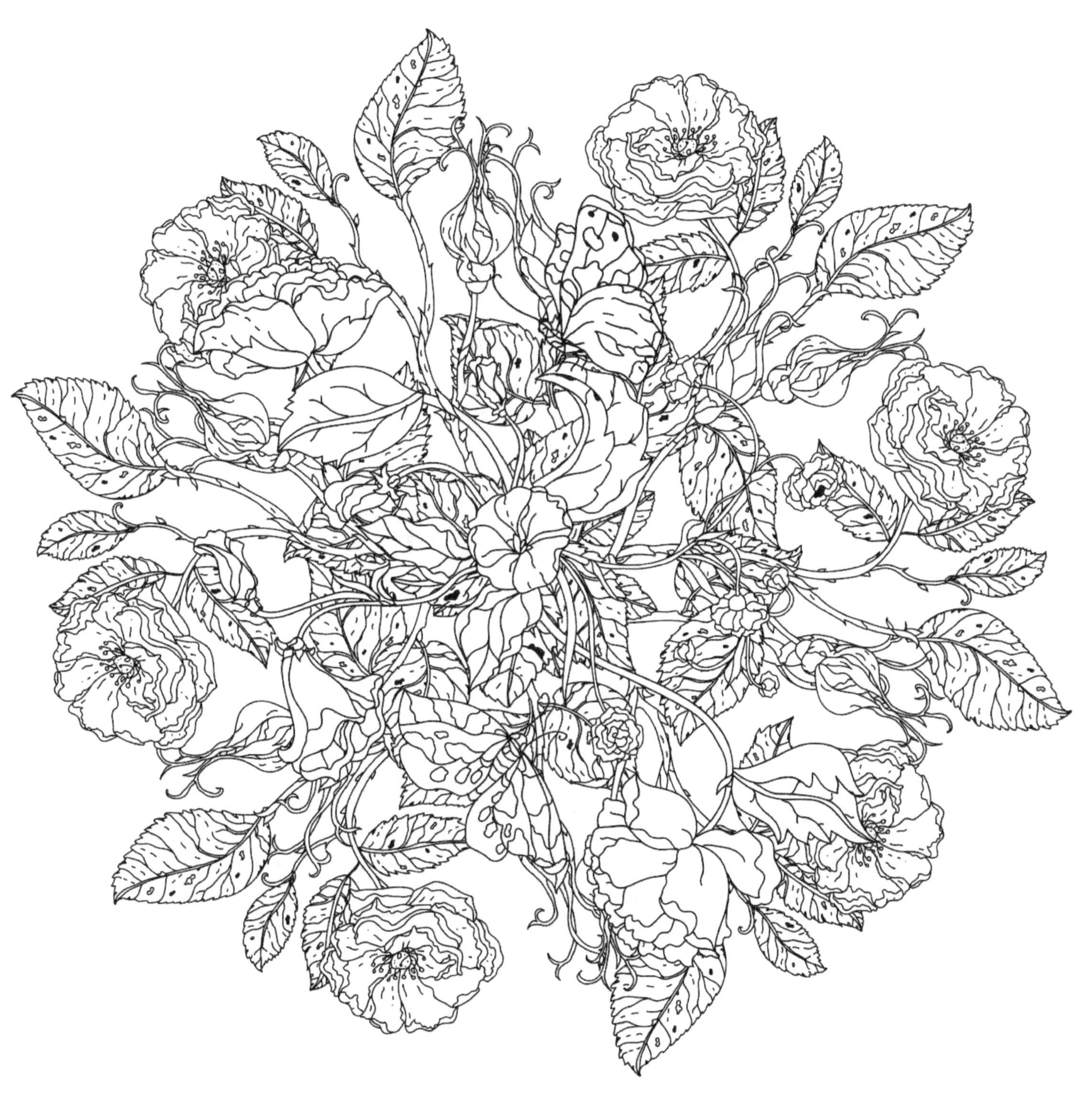

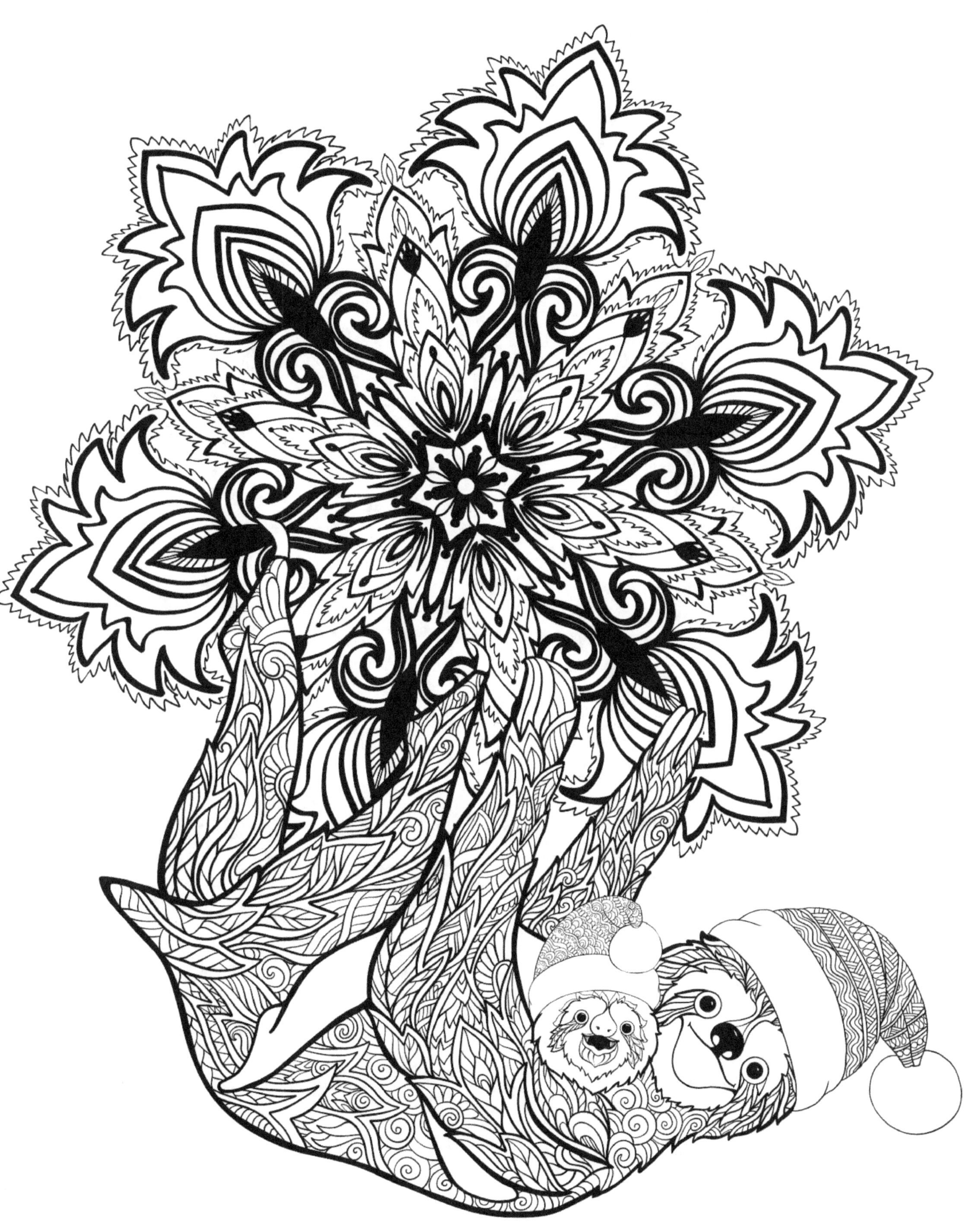

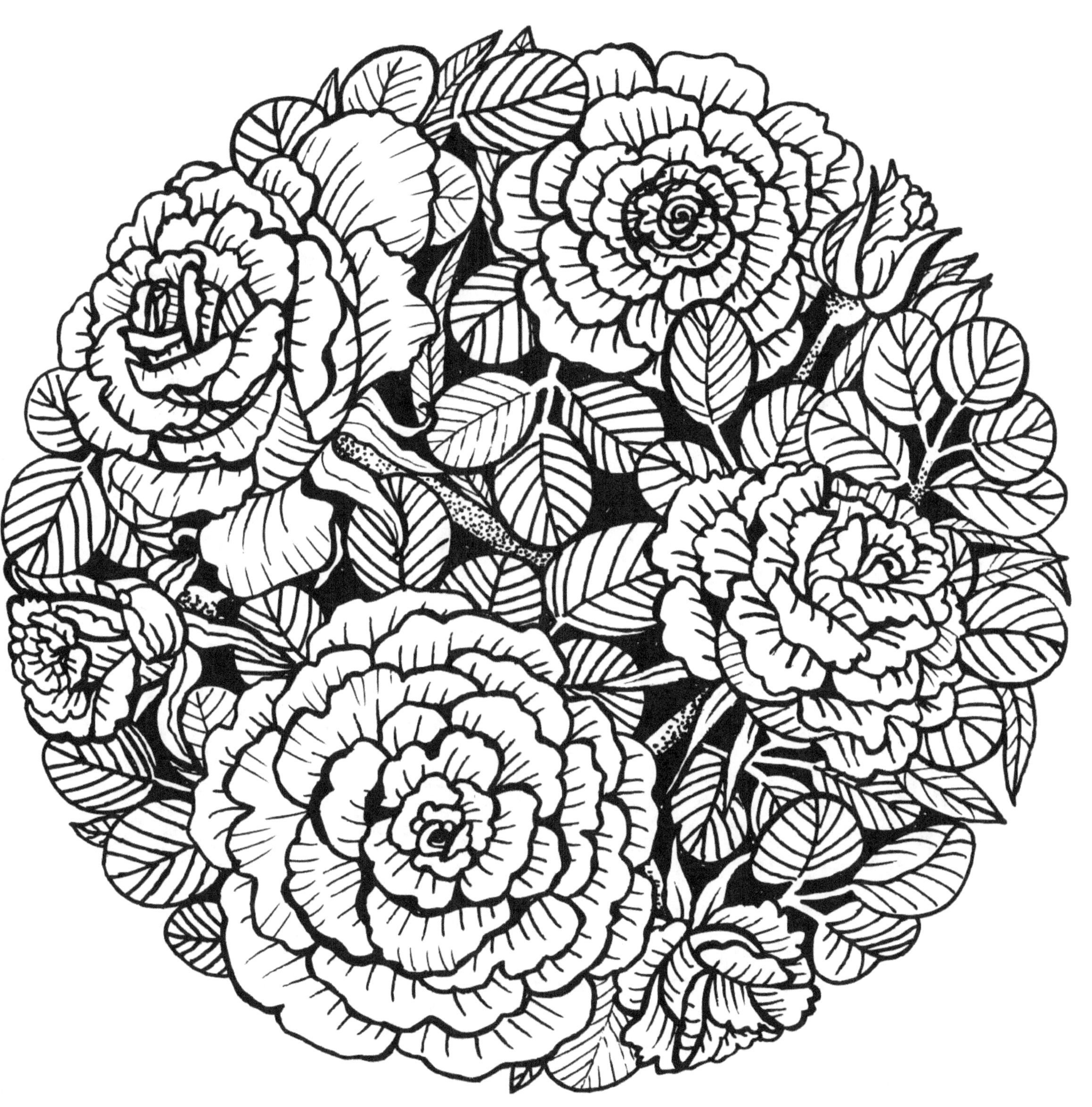

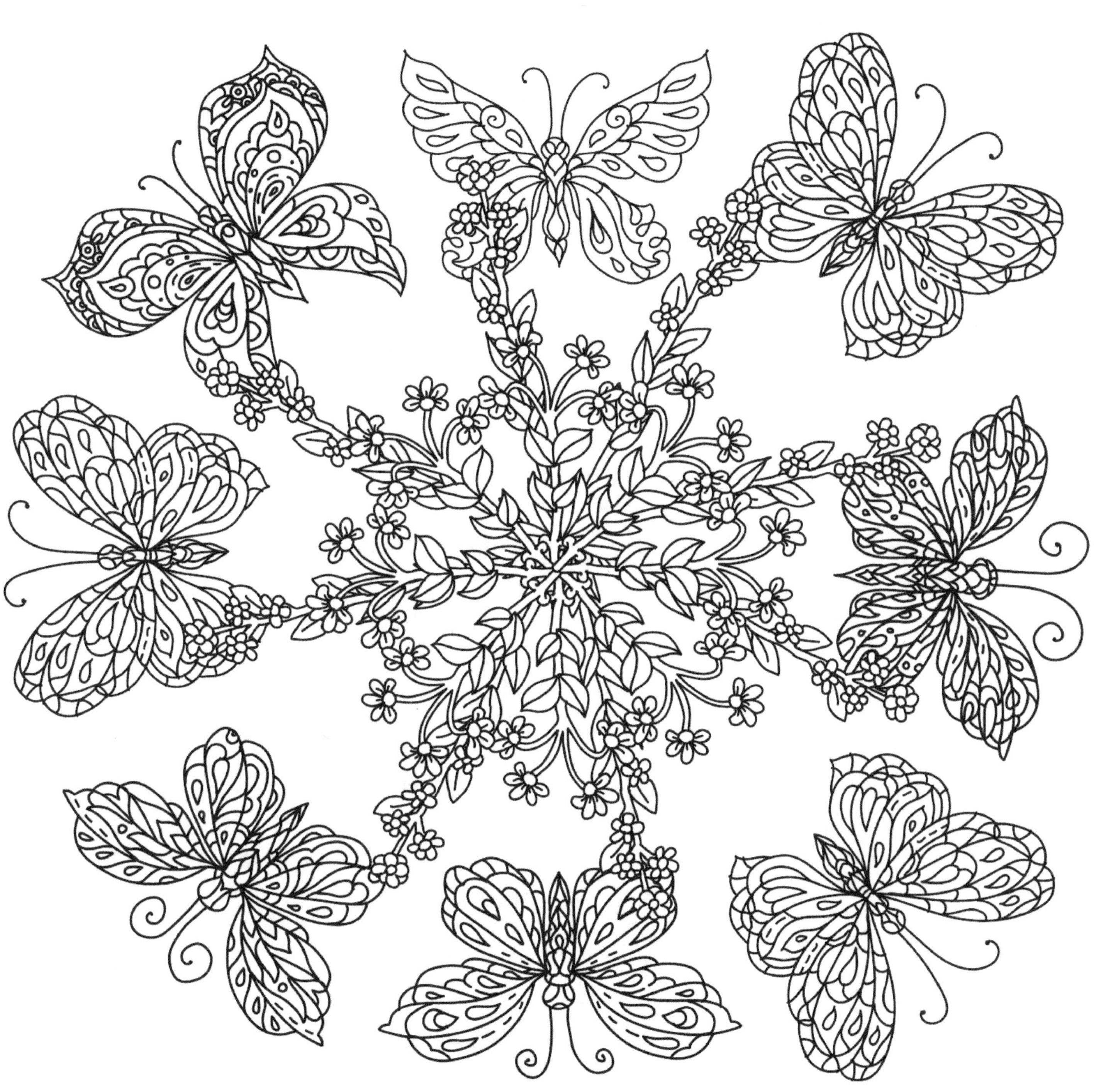

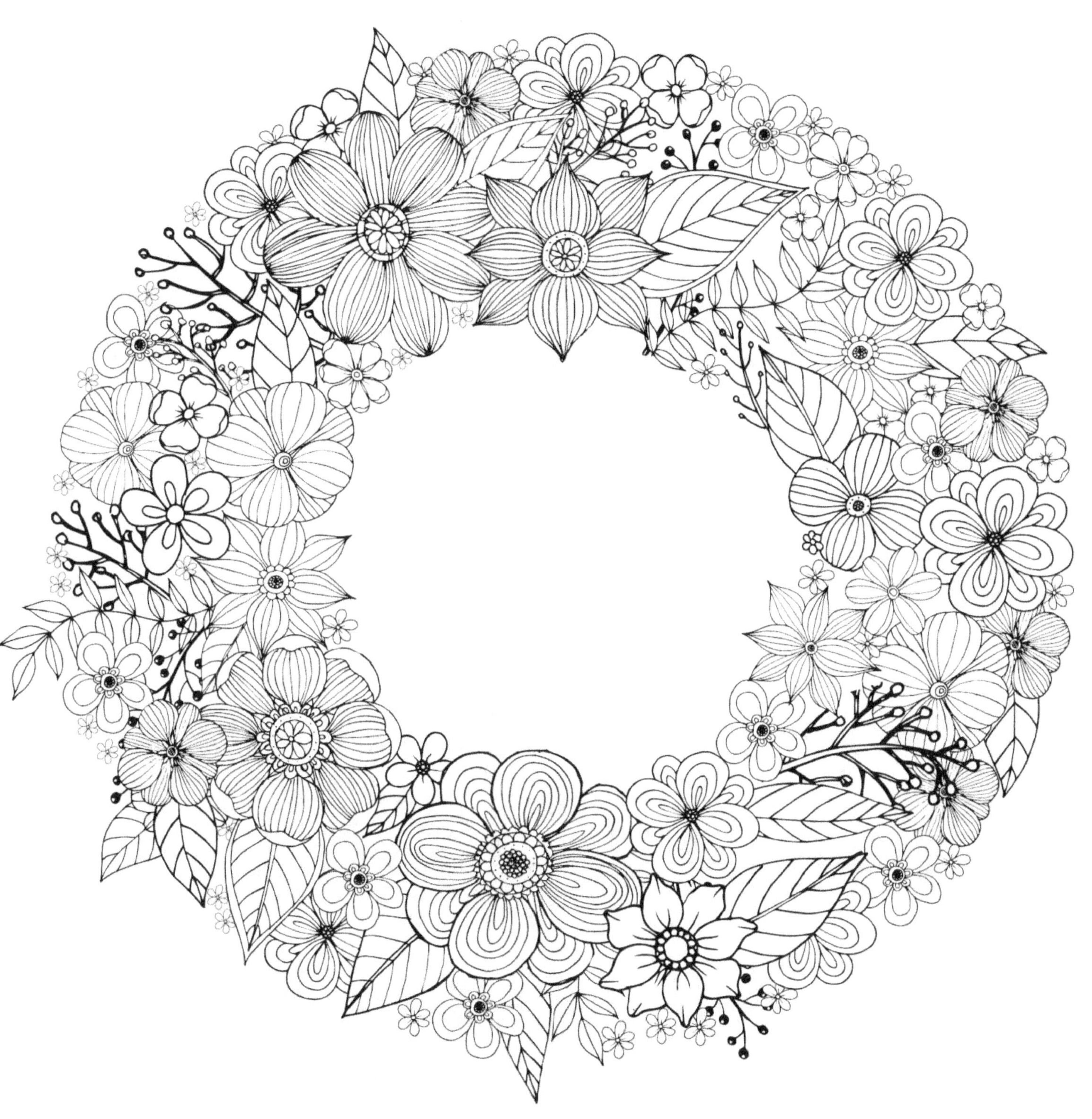

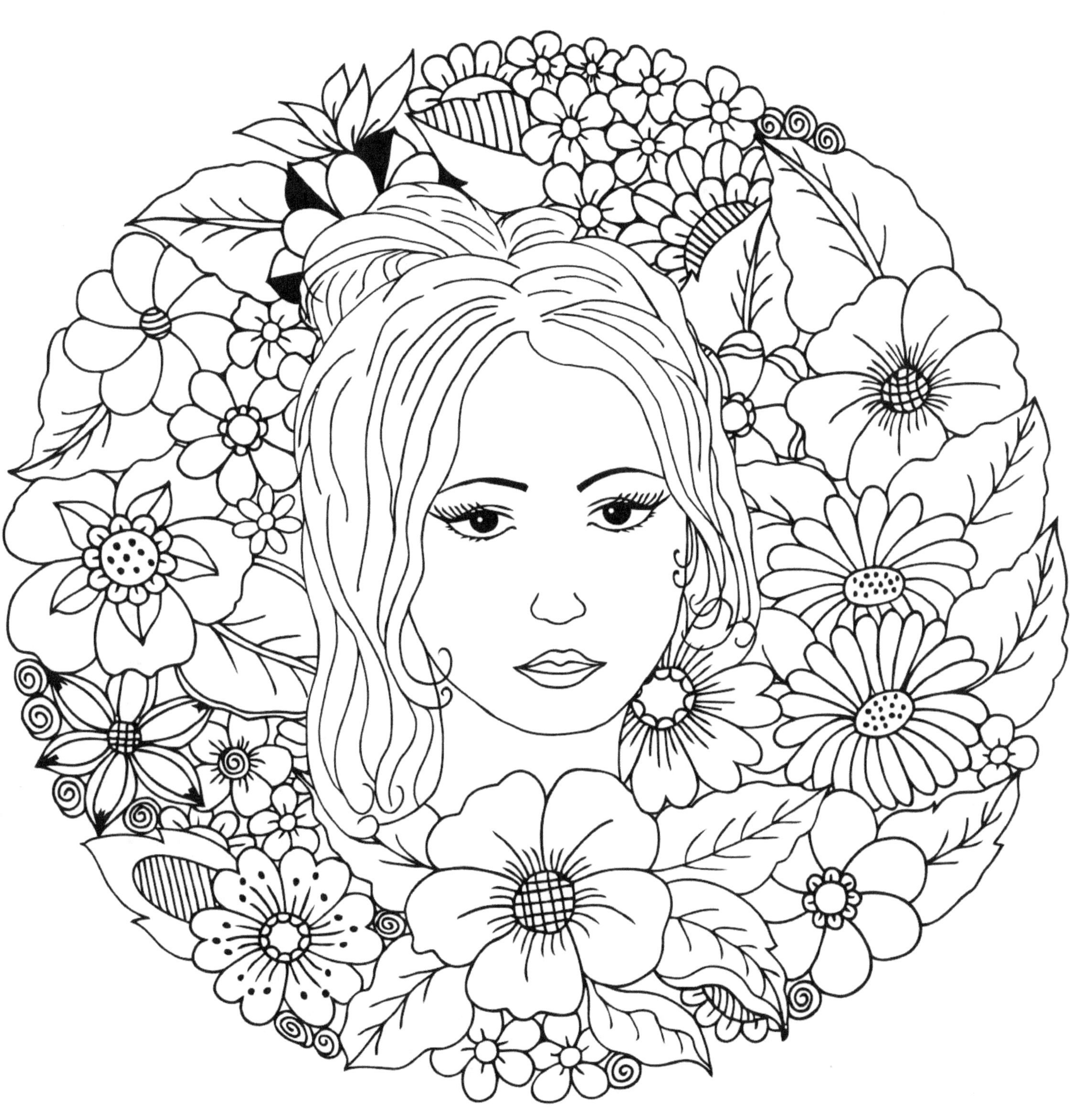

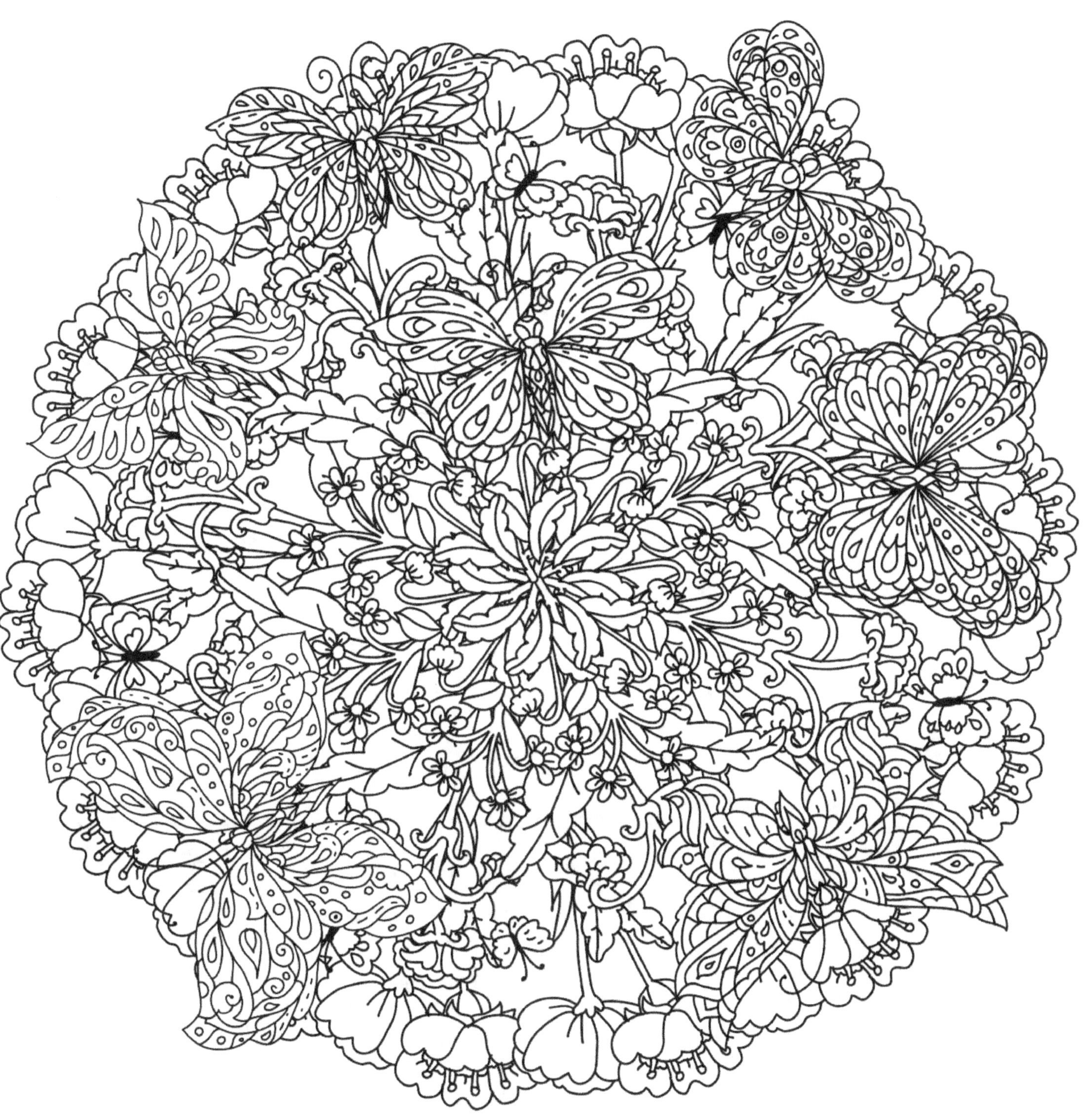